IMAGES
of America

NEVADA TEST SITE

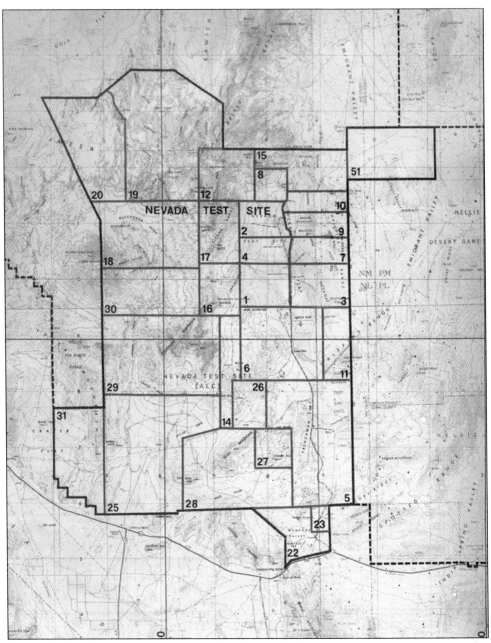

A mid-1960s map of the Nevada Test Site shows the boundaries of the numbered test areas then in use. Most of these areas were assigned numbers between 1 and 31, in no particular geographic order, and some numbers were missing entirely. A special test area established at Groom Lake in 1955 was eventually designated Area 51. (Department of Energy.)

ON THE COVER: News photographers observe an atomic detonation over Yucca Flat. Watching the atmospheric testing of nuclear explosives became a spectator sport in Nevada during the 1950s. City chambers of commerce published test schedules, hotels offered balcony and poolside viewing, and casinos served up "Atomic Cocktails" and "Miss Atom Bomb" pageants. (Las Vegas News Bureau.)

IMAGES
of America

NEVADA TEST SITE

Peter W. Merlin

ARCADIA
PUBLISHING

Published by Arcadia Publishing
Charleston, South Carolina

Printed in the United States of America

Library of Congress Control Number: 2016933100

For all general information, please contact Arcadia Publishing:
Telephone 843-853-2070
Fax 843-853-0044
E-mail sales@arcadiapublishing.com
For customer service and orders:
Toll-Free 1-888-313-2665

Visit us on the Internet at www.arcadiapublishing.com

The fiery mushroom cloud of Climax, the final shot of the 1953 test series, rises above Yucca Flat. This was a proof test of the Mk.7 high-yield, lightweight fission bomb. Dropped from a B-36 bomber, the weapon demonstrated an explosive yield equivalent to 61 kilotons of TNT conventional high explosive or three times that of Trinity, the first US atomic test. (National Nuclear Security Administration/Nevada Field Office.)

CONTENTS

ACKNOWLEDGMENTS

I have been fascinated by the history of the Nevada Test Site (NTS) and the atomic bomb since I was very young. My father had personally witnessed the devastation of Hiroshima, Japan, following the atomic bombings at the end of World War II, and growing up in the Cold War era, I regularly heard the mournful wail of the neighborhood air-raid siren as it was tested each month. Additionally, my home was located just around the corner from Lookout Mountain Laboratory, a secret film studio nestled in the Hollywood Hills, from which photographers and cinematographers ventured forth to document the nuclear weapons testing program. Many of their pictures appear in this book.

I owe a debt of gratitude to a number of individuals, as well as to numerous federal and corporate historians and archivists. I especially wish to thank Darwin Morgan and Derek Scammell for graciously providing me with their knowledge during lengthy tours of the far-flung reaches of the NTS, Alvin McLane for introducing me to the prehistoric archaeology of the Nevada Test Site, and T.D. Barnes for sharing his Area 51 archives. I offer special thanks to the outstanding people at Arcadia Publishing, including Liz Gurley, Erin Vosgien, and others without whom this project would not have been possible. Thanks, as always, to my wife, Sarah, for copy editing my draft manuscript.

Unless otherwise noted, images in this book are courtesy of the National Nuclear Security Administration/Nevada Field Office (NNSA/NV). Other sources include the US Army, US Air Force (USAF), Department of Energy (DOE), Defense Nuclear Agency (DNA), Los Alamos National Laboratory (LANL), Lawrence Livermore National Laboratory (LLNL), Lockheed Martin Skunk Works (LMSW), US Geological Survey (USGS), National Atomic Museum (NAM, later renamed the National Museum of Nuclear Science and History), National Atomic Testing Museum (NATM), National Archives and Records Administration (NARA), National Aeronautics and Space Administration (NASA), Las Vegas News Bureau, Central Intelligence Agency (CIA), and the Roadrunners Internationale (RRI) historical collection.

Those wishing to learn more about the Nevada Test Site are encouraged to visit the National Atomic Testing Museum, 755 East Flamingo Road, Las Vegas, Nevada.

INTRODUCTION

The Nevada Test Site, just 65 miles north of Las Vegas, Nevada, covers 1,573 square miles. This geographically diverse testing and training complex is the preferred location for National Nuclear Security Administration defense programs as well as other government and industry research and development efforts. For four decades, its primary purpose was developmental testing of nuclear explosives.

Atomic weapons were first developed during World War II. After a single test took place near Alamogordo, New Mexico, two atomic bombs were dropped on Japan in 1945. Seeking to better understand the effects of these new weapons, US military leaders sought a remote location where testing could be conducted under secure conditions. The first such postwar experiments took place on coral atolls more than 2,600 miles west of Hawaii. Because these operations at the Pacific Proving Ground were costly, time-consuming, and logistically difficult, officials felt it would be advisable to establish a permanent test site within the continental United States.

A top-secret feasibility study, code named Nutmeg, identified several possibilities, including the White Sands Missile Range near Alamogordo; Dugway Proving Ground, Utah; Camp Lejeune, North Carolina; and a 50-mile-wide strip between Fallon and Eureka, Nevada. The Atomic Energy Commission (AEC) ultimately selected the Las Vegas Bombing and Gunnery Range based on available space, low population density in neighboring areas, sparse annual rainfall, and the fact that the site was already under government control. Additionally, Air Force bombing and gunnery ranges bordering the site on three sides provided a buffer zone for security and public safety.

Pres. Harry S. Truman authorized the establishment of a 680-square-mile section of the range as the Nevada Proving Ground on December 18, 1950. In 1955, the name was changed to the Nevada Test Site (NTS). Land added in 1958, 1961, and 1964, the acquisition of Pahute Mesa in 1967, and a 1999 land swap with the Air Force eventually expanded the NTS to its current dimensions. In 2010, it was renamed the Nevada National Security Site (NNSS), but for the sake of consistency, it will be referred to as the NTS throughout this volume. Similarly, several national laboratories will be referred to by the names they held at the time the pictures in this book were taken.

A base camp named Mercury, located at the southernmost end and one of the few parts of the NTS visible from Highway 95, served as administrative headquarters. Though it has no permanent residents, Mercury is now the second-largest community in Nye County. The remaining parts of the NTS, known as the "forward areas," include Frenchman Flat, Yucca Flat, Rainier Mesa, Pahute Mesa, Buckboard Mesa, Plutonium Valley, and Jackass Flat. Yucca Mountain, at the southwest corner of the NTS, has been studied as a potential deep underground repository for spent nuclear fuel from commercial power plants and other high-level radioactive waste.

The entire NTS was divided into numbered areas of varying size, distributed in no particular order. Numerically, most of their numbers fall between 1 and 30, though some numbers are missing and others are out of sequence. Areas 21 and 24 are absent, and Area 13 (the site of a single safety experiment involving plutonium dispersal) is outside NTS boundaries but within the Air Force range. Area 28 no longer exists, having been absorbed into Areas 25 and 27. Rarely seen on NTS maps, a buffer zone designated Area 31 is located just west of Yucca Mountain. At one time, Area 25 was split into two areas numbered 400 and 401. In 1955, AEC spokesmen announced construction of a small airfield just off the northeast corner of the test site. Initially referred to as Watertown, it was eventually designated Area 51.

Aboveground weapons testing began on January 27, 1951, with the first of five devices dropped from B-50 bombers flying from Kirtland Air Force Base, New Mexico. These detonations, fired over Frenchman Flat in the course of just eight days, were part of Operation Ranger. At the conclusion of this first test series, the AEC began expansion of existing facilities and development of additional test areas on Yucca Flat. Construction included utility and operational structures, communications infrastructure, a forward control point, and additional personnel accommodations.

Cold War tensions between the United States and the Union of Soviet Socialist Republics (USSR) intensified after the first Soviet atomic test in 1949, spurring a race between the two superpowers to develop better and more powerful weapons that could be mass produced for ease in stockpiling. By late 1950, American designers were seeking to increase weapon yield, while reducing weight and size, and to develop safety features to prevent accidental detonation during transport and storage. Developmental prototypes and fully weaponized devices tested at the NTS were dropped from airplanes, detonated at or near ground level, fired atop steel towers, suspended from balloons, and shot from a cannon. A total of 100 atmospheric tests were conducted at the NTS through July 1962, many with the participation of thousands of Army troops and Marines to simulate the battlefield conditions of nuclear warfare and to aid in development of tactical nuclear weapons. Civil defense planners studied blast and radiation effects.

Testing of nuclear explosives in the atmosphere, in the oceans, and in space ended when the two countries signed the Limited Test Ban Treaty on August 5, 1963. Further testing was moved underground into shafts and tunnels where radioactive byproducts could be safely contained. In 1974, the Threshold Test Ban Treaty limited all nuclear explosions to yields no greater than 150 kilotons. The last underground test at the NTS took place on September 23, 1992.

Up to that time, the United States had conducted 928 tests at the NTS as well as more than a dozen at locations in Nevada, New Mexico, Colorado, Alaska, and Mississippi, plus more than 100 in the Pacific, bringing the total to 1,054. Additionally, the NTS hosted numerous non-weapons-related projects, including tests of peaceful uses for nuclear explosives (such as excavation of canals and harbors, and freeing reserves of natural gas from dense rock strata) and nuclear spacecraft propulsion experiments, and geological training for NASA's Apollo astronauts. In October 1992, the United States entered into a unilateral moratorium halting all nuclear testing. Then, in September 1996, Pres. Bill Clinton signed the Comprehensive Nuclear Test Ban Treaty with Russia (leader of the former USSR) and France, prohibiting further nuclear weapons testing. These developments did not, however, spell the end of operations at the NTS.

Today, the test site remains key to maintaining the safety and reliability of the US nuclear stockpile through subcritical experiments, those in which no self-sustaining nuclear reaction occurs. Now designated a National Environmental Research Park, this unique outdoor laboratory is where federal agencies and private industry conduct large-scale open-air experiments with hazardous and toxic chemicals and test remediation and emergency response techniques. The Department of Homeland Security conducts nuclear/radiological emergency response testing and training, and non defense research and development activities are administered in cooperation with universities, industries, and other federal agencies, ensuring that the NTS (now the NNSS) will continue to play a vital role in national security.

One

ATMOSPHERIC TESTING

An aerial view shows Camp Mercury on March 30, 1957. As the main NTS base camp, Mercury provided overnight accommodations and served as a warehousing, communication, repair, fabrication, and field administration center. The camp population was estimated at approximately 2,700 in 1955 and exploded to nearly 3,500 during the 1957 test series. The road at upper right led north to the Frenchman Flat and Yucca Flat test areas.

Facilities at Mercury included a hospital, theater, bowling alley, swimming pool, cafeteria, dormitories, and post office. Other buildings housed laboratories and instrument calibration facilities. Although Mercury is the second-largest community in Nye County, it has no schools or family housing and is operated much like a military camp due to security and work requirements.

A sign at the main security gate at Mercury identifies the test site by its early name, Nevada Proving Ground. The Atomic Energy Commission (AEC) administered the site as part of the multi-service/agency Joint Test Organization (JTO). At one time, as many as a hundred 47-passenger buses carried employees to and from Las Vegas through this gate every day. (DOE.)

All personnel were required to show identification when entering and leaving the NTS. Here, guards Milton Miller (left) and John Metcalf inspect the pass of Frank Waters, a writer with the JTO Test Information Office. NTS security guards at the time worked for Federal Services, Inc., under contract to the AEC.

A sign at the security gate reminds workers that secrecy is paramount. Test site workers had to be aware that information about their work was highly classified and restricted on a need-to-know basis. They were not authorized to share details with friends, family, and other uncleared persons. Not everyone at the NTS had a clearance, and not all clearances were equal. (DOE.)

Credentials were checked each time a person entered or exited the Administration Building or other secure area. Picture identification badges had to be worn at all times while on duty, displayed conspicuously on outer clothing. Badges or passes could not be displayed or worn outside NTS limits.

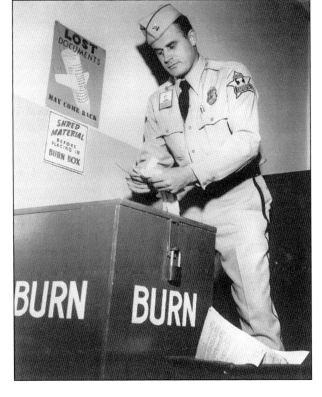

To prevent espionage, guards ensured that all discarded papers were shredded or carefully torn into tiny pieces and put into this locked box. At the end of each day, they took the box into the Incinerator Building at Mercury and burned the contents. No printed matter was to be left in wastepaper baskets.

Guards underwent extensive training in all fields of security. Here, Sgt. Marion E. Addington instructs a class on proper use and maintenance of the Thompson M1A1 submachine gun. Produced in large quantities during World War II, the .45-caliber weapon was renowned for its stopping power. Test site guards typically carried them while patrolling the perimeter and forward areas.

Marksmanship training was taken seriously at the NTS. In this 1953 photograph, guards armed with .38 Special Smith & Wesson pistols hold daily practice on the Mercury pistol range. Lt. Robert P. Keller inspects a target as Sgt. J. Brady (left) and Sgt. Marion E. Addington look on.

Female NTS workers were housed in 16 trailers at Mercury. During the 1950s, most women at the test site worked in clerical, custodial, or commissary jobs. There were relatively few female NTS employees when this picture was taken in March 1955. That year, during the Operation Teapot nuclear test series, these trailers held approximately 32 occupants.

Marilyn White, employed by the Olympic Commissary Company, emerges from a trailer home she shared with two other women employees. Olympic was responsible for housing and feeding test site workers. For White, working at the NTS was a family affair. Her husband was assigned to the Air Force Air Weather Detachment at Mercury.

Mercury initially consisted largely of temporary structures, but this changed as the test site workforce grew to 10,000. In 1962, a supplemental AEC appropriations bill included $15 million for construction of new buildings. The camp's first postal facility, established in March 1952, was replaced with a permanent post office in October 1964.

Here is the first temporary telephone switchboard at Mercury, as it looked in 1952. Public telephones for personal use were located in the Camp Services Building and the recreation hall as well as at the forward area's Control Point. The switchboard was one of the few NTS facilities staffed exclusively by women.

AEC test manager Carroll L. Tyler (left) enjoys a light moment on June 8, 1953, with William E. Ogle, Los Alamos Scientific Laboratory (LASL) deputy for weapons development, and an unidentified woman. On the chalkboard, Albert Alligator from Walt Kelly's *Pogo* comic strip says, "They is nothin more pleasant than a day with the lumps took out of it." Note the steel bear trap on top of the filing cabinet.

Recreational facilities at Mercury were originally limited to a single building with provisions for cards, pool tables, ping-pong, shuffleboard, and pinball machines. Movies were shown in a converted Quonset hut. An Olympic-sized swimming pool and eight-lane bowling alley opened in 1964. A new recreation hall also provided for badminton, square-dancing classes, and bridge tournaments.

Operation Ranger was conducted in 1951 and was the first test series to be carried out at the NTS. All five weapons were dropped from a B-50D bomber over Frenchman Flat. The first four were Mk.4 bombs (pictured) with explosive yields equivalent to between 1 and 8 kilotons of TNT high explosives, and the fifth was a 22-kiloton test of an Mk.6 bomb. (NAM.)

The distinctive stemmed fireball of an atomic blast rises above Yucca Flat following the 19-kiloton shot Dog of Operation Tumbler-Snapper, a TX-7 bomb dropped from a B-45 in May 1952. As nuclear weaponeers evaluated new design principles and test techniques, the NTS came to be known as "the Place Where the Tall Mushrooms Grow."

Here is the primary NTS Control Point, known as CP-1, as it appeared in June 1957. The largest structure at left is Control Point's main building. Beyond are a helicopter landing pad and the white expanse of Yucca Dry Lake. The smaller structure at right is the Radiological Safety Building. Parked trailers are mobile workshops of various types.

Timing and firing engineer Roger J. Pederson of contractor Edgerton, Germeshausen, and Grier (EG&G) sits at the CP-1 control panel. This was the nerve center of all nuclear test activities in Nevada. From this console, the sequence timer was activated, and here, a nuclear test could be terminated at any point up until the last moment before it was fired.

Deputy test director John C. Clark (seated) and his assistant Gaelen Felt are at the complex instrument panel in the CP-1 control room. One section of the panel was used only for airbursts, receiving signals from the bomber indicating release and, seconds later, detonation. Other panels contain frequency control equipment, with voltage recorders connected to various points in the target area and recorders for wind velocity and direction.

Although the aiming point for airdropped atomic bombs on Yucca Flat looked like a typical bull's-eye target, the weapons were actually exploded hundreds of feet above the ground. Besides giving Air Force bomber crews the opportunity to practice their weapon delivery skills, detonating nuclear devices at altitude helped minimize surface radioactivity. (DNA.)

During a pre-shot evaluation meeting, program directors report on the readiness of experiments, weathermen forecast meteorological conditions for the next day's shot time, blast experts forecast on-site and off-site effects, and radiation experts predict the amount and dispersal of fallout. A panel of governmental experts in public health, medicine, radiation, blast, and weather then evaluates all conditions and recommends to the test manager whether or not to fire.

Precise weather forecasting was of primary importance in atomic testing. To obtain information concerning air pressure, temperature, and humidity, these captive, helium-filled Kytoon balloons, supplied by the USAF Air Weather Service, were sent aloft before each nuclear test, and hauled down minutes before detonation. Last-minute weather information was relayed by remote control to the AEC test director at the Control Point.

During test operations, Air Force personnel tracked and coordinated aircraft movement from the Air Control Center at Indian Springs using radar scopes and plotting boards. As many as 40 aircraft at a time were aloft for weather reconnaissance, observation, particulate sampling, aerial photography, dropping test weapons, or participating in military training exercises.

Air Force technical sergeant Richardson uses a plotting board to keep track of aircraft over the test site. The board was marked with a polar coordinate grid printed on it and a distance scale. With this simple tool, air controllers could not only plot the track of aerial targets but also solve problems in relative motion through use of vector algebra.

Everett F. Cox (left), head of the JTO Blast Prediction Unit, and Jack Reed use a Raypac "electronic brain" developed by the AEC Sandia Laboratory in Albuquerque. The Raypac, short for Ray Path Analog Computer, was used to predict, record, and compute blast effects as far as 135 miles from the test site. It performed calculations in a fraction of the time needed for manual computation.

Following a test, Willard A. Gustafson of Sandia checks a recorder tape to determine at what time and with what intensity the blast wave, originating 100 miles away in the Nevada Test Site, disturbed the atmospheric pressure at Boulder City Airport. Calculations were made using data on wind speed and direction, air temperature, burst altitude, and other factors.

The flash of a nuclear explosion creates a false dawn over the downtown Las Vegas skyline. Capitalizing on the atomic spectacle, the Las Vegas Chamber of Commerce printed calendars advertising detonation times and viewing locations. Casinos like Binion's Horseshoe and the Desert Inn offered "atomic cocktails" and Bomb Parties. Showgirls at the Sands, costumed as mushroom clouds, vied for the title of "Miss Atomic Bomb." (Las Vegas News Bureau.)

Don English, a photographer for the Las Vegas News Bureau, captured this image overlooking Fremont Street from the roof of the Golden Nugget Hotel and Casino. When workmen installing a glass skylight asked him what he was doing, he told them they would know shortly. He was not kidding. After the bomb went off, the ground began to shake, and several panes of glass broke. (Las Vegas News Bureau.)

Photographers from the Air Force Lookout Mountain Laboratory (LML) in Hollywood, California, operate multiple cameras from the back of a C-47 with the cargo door removed. These cameramen recorded data in both motion and still pictures that were later studied and used in the evaluation of weapons effects tests and the gathering of scientific test data.

An LML film crew holds onto its cameras as the blast shock wave hits. Observers located several miles from ground zero would not hear or feel the blast for as much as 20 or 30 seconds after detonation. This phenomenon often took the uninitiated quite by surprise. This picture was taken at the exact moment of shock wave arrival.

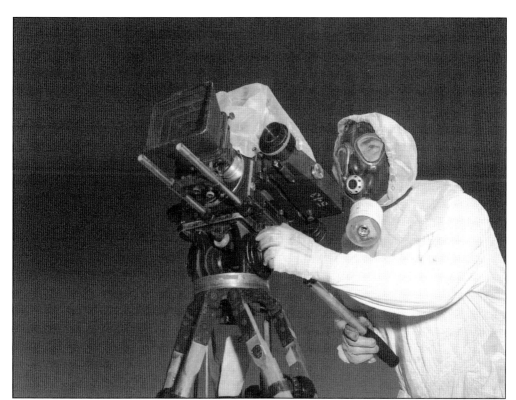

LML photographer Air Force staff sergeant John Kelly prepares to film an atomic explosion. Note that he is wearing protective gear and has even covered the camera's film magazine. The Air Force established the 1352nd Photographic Squadron (later Motion Picture Group) at LML in 1948 to produce still and motion picture photography in support of the Department of Defense and AEC. (LANL.)

Photographers from LML document the 3.2-kiloton Wasp Prime airdrop on March 29, 1955. This was a repeat of an earlier test of the Wasp design, using a higher yield core for weapons development purposes. This shot was fired five hours after Apple-1, the first time in US history that two nuclear explosions were set off on the same day.

An atomic mushroom cloud rises above Yucca Flat on April 22, 1952, following shot Charlie of Operation Tumbler-Snapper. More than 1,500 civilian observers, news media, soldiers, and paratroopers in the air witnessed the 31-kiloton airburst over Area 7. This event was the first atomic bomb test to be televised live. (DOE.)

Among the reporters who covered Charlie, also known as "Operation Big Shot," were United Press correspondents, from left to right, Frank M. Bartholomew, Robert N. Bennyhoff, Joe Quinn, and Hugh Baille. Prior to this time, such events had not been announced in advance but pressure from the public and media forced the AEC to do so. (Library of Congress.)

Photographers perch on rocks northeast of the Control Point. The rocky outcrop, was dubbed "News Nob" in 1952 after construction worker Tom Sherrod placed a weather-beaten board with a doorknob attached—supposedly from an outdoor privy—and painted the name across it in yellow letters. The original board was later replaced with a more professional-looking commemorative sign. (Las Vegas News Bureau.)

Newsmen watch a predawn detonation from News Nob in 1953. The fading fireball suffused the mushroom cloud with an eerie purple glow. Ragged parallel lines to the left of the cloud's stem are smoke trails from sounding rockets launched seconds before detonation to create reference lines against which the progress of the shock front could be photographed. (NAM.)

Camp Desert Rock, located two miles south of Mercury, was established by the Army in 1951 and accommodated members of all four military services participating in training exercises that included observing atomic explosions from trenches as close as a quarter mile from ground zero and executing simulated military maneuvers. (US Army.)

With 100 semi-permanent buildings and more than 500 tents, the camp could accommodate as many as 6,000 people. In a 1951 orientation guide, Col. Loren D. Buttoph, officer in charge, declared, "We realize that the accommodations offered here are not equal to those of the Excelsior Hotels of [Europe] or the Grand Hotels of the Far East, but they are Camp Desert Rock's Best." (NATM.)

Army troops rehearse moving into slit trenches in preparation for a shot during Operation Teapot, the 1955 test series. Each trench was six feet deep and less than three feet wide. This one was located approximately 4,000 yards from ground zero. These soldiers wore no special protective gear beyond their regular uniforms.

Soldiers hunker down in their trench prior to a shot during Exercise Desert Rock VI. The Desert Rock exercises were conducted in conjunction with full-scale nuclear tests in order to develop tactical concepts and techniques relating to atomic warfare and to acclimate personnel to the environment of an atomic battlefield.

Lt. Gen. John R. Hodge, chief of Army Field Forces, joined congressional observers and 6th Army troops in observation trenches 7,000 yards from ground zero on June 1, 1952. The 15-kiloton test of a TX-5 weapon took place atop a tower north of Yucca Dry Lake. From left to right are Hodge and US representatives Errett P. Schrivner of Kansas and Daniel J. Flood of Pennsylvania.

Illuminated by the flash of the 43-kiloton shot Simon on April 25, 1953, Army combat troops crouch in their narrow trench awaiting the shock wave. The brilliant, soundless glare was followed seconds later by a terrific concussion and a deep rumbling. Dust and debris rained down on the assembled soldiers for several minutes.

Army soldiers kneel with their backs to the blast, covering their eyes against the bright flash. Some later reported being able to see the bones in their arms despite having their eyes shut. Even several miles away, they felt the terrific heat and powerful shock wave. When they turned around, the troops saw hillsides aflame and the fiery mushroom cloud roiling into the sky.

Soldiers emerge from trenches and prepare to advance following the Encore shot on May 8, 1953. Dropped from a B-50, the bomb exploded 2,400 feet over Frenchman Flat with a yield of 27 kilotons. Over the ensuing hours, more than 2,000 troops in battalion combat teams attacked two simulated objectives and toured a display of military equipment within the blast zone.

Second Lt. Allen Price leads a platoon of men from B Company, 167th Regiment, 31st Infantry Division, toward the blast area while checking the intensity of the radiation in the area with a radiac meter. Price participated in the exercise as a member of the 6th Army Chemical, Biological, and Radiological School.

Pfc. Carl Lacinaki (right) hands his film dosimeter badge to Lt. Pearle W. Mack so that it may be checked for radiation exposure during Operation Tumbler-Snapper in 1952. Lacinaki was an assistant gunner of a 75-millimeter (mm) recoilless rifle with the 31st Infantry Division. Mack was assigned as Chemical-Biological-Radiological officer of the 373rd Transportation Port Battalion.

Members of the Army's 82nd Airborne Division parachute into the area near ground zero immediately following Tumbler-Snapper shot Charlie. Lessons learned during Desert Rock exercises helped Army planners develop the concept of the Pentomic Division, a combination of infantry and airborne divisions capable of waging warfare on a nuclear battlefield.

A machine gun crew gazes at a predawn atomic cloud. Military officials recognized that soldiers might be overwhelmed by the sights and sounds generated by an atomic bomb, the stress felt in the moments leading up to the blast, and while maneuvering on the atomic battlefield. Many tests involving troop maneuvers included studies by psychologists, sociologists, and physiologists from various institutions.

Like the sun come down to Earth, an atomic fireball expands over an array of tanks, trucks, and other military equipment. The shock wave is clearly visible ahead of the fireball's edge and reflecting off the desert below. Combination of the primary wave with the reflected wave dramatically increased the blast overpressure and the bomb's destructive force.

A radiological survey team examines the remains of a radar van and trailer following an atomic bomb shot detonated on May 1, 1952. Under the direction of the Desert Rock control group, observers toured this display area to see the effects of the blast on equipment and prepared positions. Radiation measurements determined the limits of safe advance.

34

A soldier inspects a damaged truck that had been placed at a position between 400 and 500 yards from ground zero during shot Charlie of Operation Tumbler-Snapper in 1952. Gen. Harry P. Storke, the exercise director, believed the use of tactical atomic weapons would not significantly alter combat tactics, with the exception of adding radiological safety precautions.

Sgt. George Underwood (left) and radiological safety officer lieutenant Fred D. McFadden consider the condition of a dummy in full combat gear at an unsheltered position 1,700 yards from ground zero. Display areas such as this provided opportunities to gauge the reaction of the troops as well as to understand the effects of the blast on military equipment.

A flight of Sikorsky HRS-1 helicopters from Marine Medium Helicopter Squadron 363 wings its way over the NTS during a training flight on March 17, 1955. A few days later, 30 of these helicopters airlifted Marines from various assembly points immediately after a detonation to execute tactical maneuvers in the shadow of the atomic cloud.

Following arrival at Camp Desert Rock aboard a transport helicopter, a bulldog named Maggie served as the Marine mascot during Operation Teapot. For the duration of the exercise, she was dubbed "Sergeant Roentgen" (a roentgen is one unit of radiation). Bulldogs had traditionally served as Marine Corps mascots since 1922.

Marines of the 4th Provisional Atomic Exercise Brigade practice combat maneuvers in advance of shot Hood of Operation Plumbbob in 1957. The device was to be detonated at the top of the steel tower in the background. During the shot, some Marines were stationed in trenches as close as 5,700 yards from ground zero. (Dave Cicero.)

Marines prepare to leave their foxhole and advance toward an atomic mushroom cloud during Exercise Desert Rock IV, part of Operation Tumbler-Snapper in 1952. Two battalions consisting of 1,950 Marines from Camp Pendleton, California, and Camp Lejeune, North Carolina, maneuvered through the blast area following the 19-kiloton shot while other observers remained behind in trenches.

Donald Ott and Sara Beth Hawkins of the Biomedical Research Group at LASL place laboratory mice into a blast-resistant metal container at Yucca Flat in May 1957. Protected against blast, heat, and shock, similar containers were placed at various distances from ground zero during shot Franklin of Operation Plumbbob to study radiation exposure in animals.

A 25-pound shoat is removed from an aluminum barrel by Staff Sgt. Nathaniel Morgan, 47th Field Hospital, Fort Sam Houston, Texas, following shot Franklin. The containers were positioned at various distances from ground zero to measure radiation doses as part of a series of medical effects tests. The shoat was one of 1,200 swine bred especially for the test.

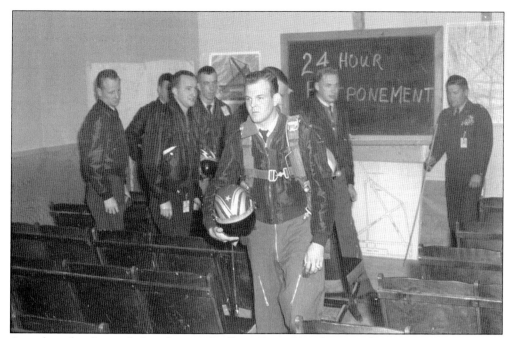

A predawn briefing at Indian Springs Air Force Base, 20 miles east of Camp Desert Rock, ends in disappointment. Lt. Col. James A. Watkins (right) has just informed pilots of the 4926th Test Squadron (Sampling) of a last-minute postponement of the first shot in the 1955 test series. Such delays resulted in hours of additional work for maintenance men and aircrews.

Navy lieutenant F.E. Evans (left) discusses positioning techniques with Cdr. John E. Tefft, project officer from the Naval Air Special Weapons Facility, Albuquerque, New Mexico. The unit operated specially instrumented Douglas AD-4 Skyraiders flying data-collecting missions as close to ground zero at shot time as safety permitted. Note that Evans is wearing anti-flash goggles.

The largest airplane to take part in Operation Teapot was the Convair B-36, a hybrid of World War II and Jet Age technologies. On April 6, 1955, a B-36 crew assigned to the 4925th Test Group (Atomic) at Kirtland Air Force Base, New Mexico, dropped an atomic weapon from 42,000 feet over the western edge of Yucca Flat. (USAF.)

Capt. William L. Hickey of the 4925th Test Group (Atomic) concentrates on the controls of his B-36 bomber. The bomb he dropped was a test device to investigate its use as an air-to-air antiaircraft missile warhead. It detonated at 36,620 feet with an explosive force of 3.2 kilotons and was parachute-retarded to slow its fall so that the bomber could escape any blast effects.

During Operation Teapot, Maj. James T. Corn flew a B-57A jet bomber through atomic clouds over Nevada to measure radiation. In 1953, Corn and Lt. William H. Wright flew a similar jet to an altitude of 54,000 feet to collect samples from a Soviet atomic test. Corn is seen here wearing a David Clark Company S-2 capstan-type partial-pressure suit and K-1 helmet for protection at high altitude.

This sleek Boeing B-47 Stratojet medium bomber was among numerous aircraft participating in Operation Teapot. Twenty-nine of the six-engine Stratojets, which could fly higher and faster than any bomber in their class, were flown as support aircraft during various shots. Although capable of dropping nuclear weapons, most of them were RB-47 reconnaissance types used for photographic missions.

Air Force major Edward S. Stahl prepares to take off from Indian Springs. A wide variety of Air Force and Navy planes took part in Operation Teapot for the purpose of weapons drop, observation, and aerial sampling of radioactive clouds and fallout. Aircrews were equipped with dosimeter badges to measure exposure to radiation.

Air Force officers study flash-blindness by observing the initial intense light of an atomic burst through specially coated aircraft windows and then recording their individual reactions using the equipment shown. These experiments began in 1951 with volunteers circling in a C-54 at an altitude of 15,000 feet approximately nine miles from the atomic blast. Test subjects were exposed to three detonations, after which changes in their visual acuity were measured.

A QF-80 jet drone (upper left; note the empty cockpit) is shown in takeoff position at Indian Springs for a pilotless sampling mission through a radioactive cloud on April 6, 1953. The drone was remotely controlled by a pilot in the back seat of the DT-33 in the foreground. This marked the first use of jet drones during continental nuclear tests.

An airman at Indian Springs uses a high-pressure hose to wash a T-33 drone (similar to the earlier QF-80). Drones were used to collect airborne particulate samples and sometimes carried monkeys or mice for biomedical research purposes. After each flight, sampling aircraft were decontaminated with a mixture of a grease solvent and water in order to reduce possible radiation hazards to ground crew.

Not all sampling missions involved drones. An Air Force crew flew this WB-29 through the atomic cloud following shot Charlie in April 1952. After landing at Indian Springs, airmen wearing gloves, rubber boots, and air-filter masks washed the airplane down. Note the sample collection box on the bottom of the wing near the outboard engine.

After the WB-29 has been washed and allowed to sit for a while, radiological safety monitors staff sergeant T.B. Davis and corporal J.E. Bell check radiation levels to determine whether it is safe for maintenance men or aircrews to approach. Note that other than rubber boots and cotton gloves, these men are not wearing any special protective gear.

Upon returning to Indian Springs after gathering air samples from an atomic cloud, a Republic F-84G sampling aircraft is guided into the decontamination area. The plane will be left in this segregated parking area until radioactivity has decreased to a nonhazardous level. Wingtip pods equipped with special filters were used to collect samples of radioactive particulates.

A2c. Thomas O. Summers removes a particulate-collection filter from a wingtip pod on an F-84G belonging to the 4926th Test Squadron (Sampling). Summers was a member of the squadron's five-man Filter Recovery Section, the only organization of its kind in the Air Force. Note the long-handled pole used to limit his radiation exposure.

A plume of rocket smoke partially obscures a Northrop F-89J flown by Capt. Eric W. Hutchison and Capt. Alfred C. Barbee on July 19, 1957. Shot John of Operation Plumbbob was the first and only firing of a live nuclear-armed antiaircraft missile. At a signal from the ground, the unguided rocket exploded at an altitude of 18,500 feet.

The Genie missile's nuclear warhead exploded with a yield of 1.7 kilotons. It was visible from Indian Springs, some 30 miles away from the point of detonation. Another F-89J, sister ship of the launching aircraft, is visible in the foreground. Test officials said that the operation was fully successful, and that no fallout, other than negligible traces, was reported by off-site AEC radiological monitors.

Five officers from Continental Air Defense Command (pictured) and LML photographer technical sergeant George Yoshitake observed shot John while standing directly underneath the airburst without helmets, hats, caps, goggles, or protective clothing, to illustrate that the civil populace need fear no harmful effects should it be necessary to use the atomic rockets in tactical situations.

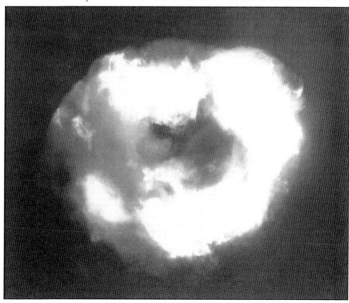

John left an unusual orange smoke ring swirling above Yucca Flat. This phenomenon was described on camera by the volunteer observers, who included Col. Sidney C. Bruce, Lt. Col. Frank P. Ball, Maj. John W. Hughes II, Maj. Norman Bodinger, and Maj. Donald A. Lutrell. As the official documentarian, Technical Sergeant Yoshitake was the only non-volunteer.

Some nuclear explosive devices were placed inside sheet metal cabs atop steel towers ranging from 100 to 700 feet in height. The nearby array of five thin towers was used to support instruments for measuring fireball temperatures. The automobile at lower left was one of a number of target vehicles placed at varying distances from ground zero to study blast effects.

Depending on explosive yield, nuclear explosions did not always vaporize the shot towers. Some of the smaller shots merely reduced the steel structures to piles of twisted and melted debris. Because residual radioactivity around the base of the tower prevented getting a close-up photograph, this picture was shot with a telephoto lens.

This is one of four 500-foot steel towers used in the Teapot series. Increased height meant that less particulate matter would be drawn up into the atomic cloud and that there would be less fallout off-site. The cost of fabricating and erecting each of these towers was approximately $154,000 in 1955.

This 700-foot tower for shot Smoky in 1957 was among the highest constructed for an atomic test. These towers were designed to contain as little metal as possible, partly for economy but primarily to reduce the quantity of vaporized material contributing to radioactive fallout. The elevator is visible about halfway up to the shot cab.

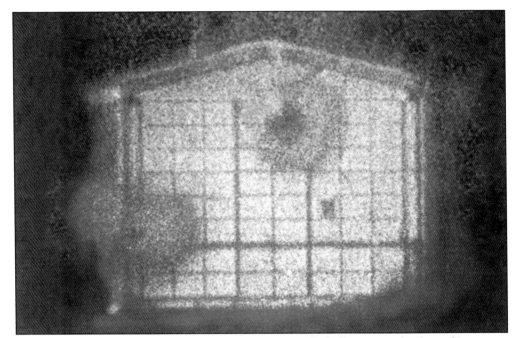

In the earliest moments of a nuclear explosion, a brilliant flash illuminates the shot cab's interior. A light brighter than 100 suns reveal steel framework through corrugated tin siding that is just beginning to vaporize under intense X-ray bombardment. Images like this could be captured only with specialized ultrahigh-speed cameras developed by EG&G. (NAM.)

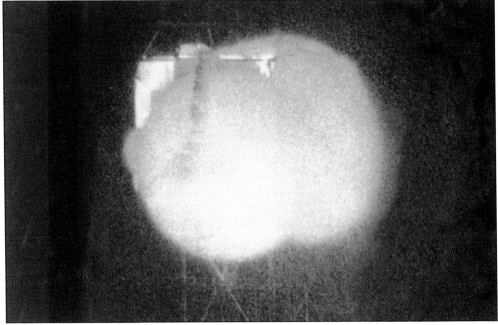

The fireball begins to consume the shot cab in an image captured by a rapatronic camera, so named because of its rapid-action electronic shutter. Dr. Harold Edgerton, a pioneer in strobe photography, developed the concept in the 1940s. Along with his partners at EG&G, he later developed special magneto-optical cameras for capturing the development of atomic explosions. (LANL.)

This rapatronic image shows the 19-kiloton shot Whitney of Operation Plumbbob on September 23, 1957. Note that although the shot cab and upper portion of the 500-foot tower have been engulfed, the supporting guy wires have not yet had time to recoil. Capturing the earliest moments of atomic explosions was exceptionally challenging, not only because of the extraordinary light intensity but also due to the brief duration of associated phenomena. Exposure time for rapatronic images was just one hundred-millionth of a second. Such fast exposure times made it impossible to use a conventional mechanical shutter system. Instead, a magnetic field was created around two polarized lenses that were rotated, permitting light to pass through an optical system. Due to the deleterious effects of shock waves and radiation on camera equipment, the rapatronic camera was positioned several miles from ground zero. (DOE.)

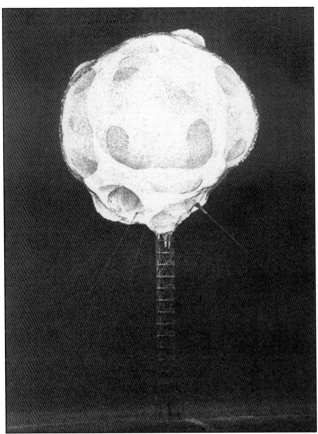

Within 0.0001 seconds of detonation, the 32-kiloton shot Harry of Operation Upshot-Knothole on May 19, 1953, has consumed nearly half the height of its 300-foot tower. Surface irregularity is the result of high-velocity bomb debris splashing against the backside of the shock front, which is expanding slightly more slowly than the debris and glows due to compression heating of the surrounding air. (DOE.)

One of the most unusual phenomena revealed by rapatronic imaging was dubbed the "rope trick effect" by physicist John Malik. Peculiar spikes protruding from the bottom of the fireball resulted from the heating, rapid vaporization, and expansion of guy wires and instrumentation cables extending from the shot cab to the ground. (DOE.)

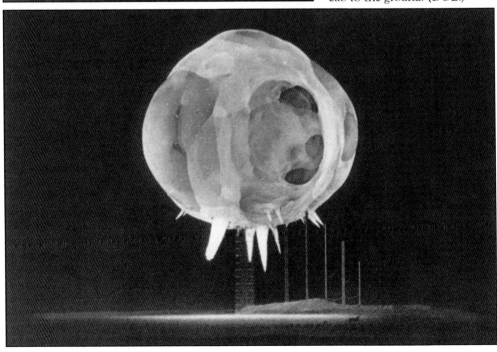

By the time this image was taken on June 5, 1952, the 14-kiloton explosion had completely enveloped its tower. Researchers observed that when cables and guy wires were painted black spike formation was enhanced, but if they were coated with reflective paint or wrapped in aluminum foil, no spikes were observed. (DOE.)

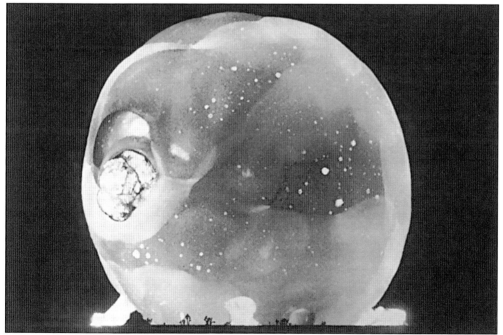

An atomic fireball dwarfs a stand of Joshua trees as the expanding shock front contacts the ground, the final stage before formation of the mushroom cloud. Since each rapatronic camera could record only one image on a sheet of film, banks of 4 to 10 cameras were set up to take image sequences documenting fireball development. (DOE.)

On the morning of January 30, 1957, technicians prepare to raise a moored balloon at one of the firing areas on Yucca Flat. At this time, Nevada Test Organization and Sandia personnel were beginning a series of experiments to determine whether anchored balloons could be used as detonation platforms for full-scale nuclear tests.

With a dummy load simulating the weight of a nuclear device, a test balloon begins its ascent. Tethered to the ground by steel cables, the balloon could be raised to desired altitudes up to 1,500 feet. Eliminating the need for steel towers and being able to fire nuclear devices at much higher elevations above the ground alleviated radioactive fallout.

Shot Grable of Operation Upshot-Knothole on May 25, 1953, tested a nuclear artillery shell. Fired from a 280-mm cannon, the projectile was programmed to detonate 1,500 feet above a target six miles away. It exploded at a third of that height with a yield of 15 kilotons. Ground zero was the center of the dry lake bed on Frenchman Flat.

A soldier inspects the 280-mm cannon, nicknamed "Atomic Annie," immediately following shot Grable. Army officials wanted to demonstrate the weapon under realistic tactical conditions. After artillery crewmen loaded the armed nuclear projectile into the cannon's breech and set explosive charges, they retreated to nearby trenches while the weapon was fired by an electronic signal from CP-1. (DNA.)

In an exercise that news outlets dubbed "Operation Doorstep," the Federal Civil Defense Administration (FCDA) constructed two houses on Yucca Flat that were representative of those found in a typical American community. This picture shows a wood-frame house, located 3,500 feet from ground zero, at the moment of detonation on March 17, 1953.

Heat from the 16-kiloton shot Annie sets fire to the front of the house. To evaluate blast effects, a high-speed motion picture camera captured the destruction at 24 frames per second. The 35-mm camera was protected from radiation by a two-inch-thick lead enclosure, and the atomic detonation provided the only light source.

The charred front wall begins to buckle and roof tiles are stripped away as the blast wave hits. The flames had already self-extinguished. Evidently, the thermal radiation dropped off before sufficient heat was generated to sustain a fire. There were no thermal effects inside the house. All other structural damage resulted from the shock wave.

Total destruction begins two seconds after detonation as the house begins to disintegrate. The roof is torn off, the brick chimney collapses, and the air is filled with debris. Only the basement area survived with relatively little damage. FCDA officials concluded that basement shelters would provide substantial protection to occupants.

In another test house, located 7,500 feet from ground zero, mannequins are arranged to represent a typical family scene. Every effort was made to replicate the interior of a suburban home. The FCDA obtained the mannequins at no cost from the L.A. Darling Company of Bronson, Michigan; J.C. Penney provided clothing; Atlas Trucking donated hauling services and some items of furniture.

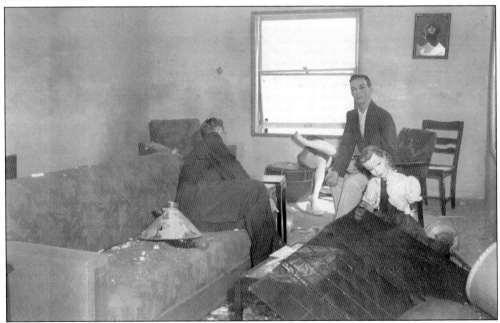

After the blast, some mannequins appear to be comparatively undisturbed, though the upright male had plaster chipped from both eyes and the little girl was severely marked around the forehead. Most injuries in this house would have resulted from flying debris and window glass. Initial radiation effects would have been negligible.

A mannequin family waits for the atomic burst inside a basement shelter 7,500 feet from ground zero. This box-type shelter, constructed from heavy timbers, was called a "corner room" because it was built into a corner of the basement with cinder block or concrete walls on two sides. Note that the shelter has been stocked with Civil Defense supplies.

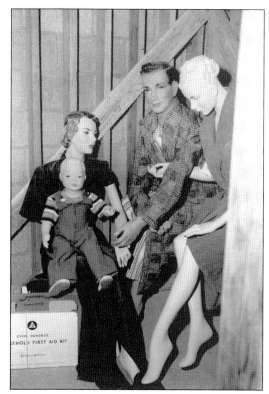

Most home handymen in 1953 could build a lean-to shelter like this with about $40 worth of materials. This picture was taken before the 16-kiloton shot on March 17, 1953. Even after the house 3,500 feet from ground zero was blasted from its foundation, mannequins inside this type of shelter were undamaged.

FCDA volunteers enjoy coffee and doughnuts during Operation Cue, a full-fledged Civil Defense exercise in May 1955. During this exercise, which coincided with the 29-kiloton Apple-2 shot, FCDA personnel completed 40 projects to evaluate effects of nuclear detonations on civilian communities and test the emergency response capabilities of Civil Defense organizations. (NARA.)

An FCDA volunteer from Kansas surveys damage in a house 4,700 feet from ground zero. The agency constructed a representation of a typical American community complete with homes, utility services, automobiles, furniture, appliances, food, and mannequins. Nearly 300 Civil Defense workers participated in a post-shot field exercise focusing on measures necessary to rehabilitate a town following a nuclear strike. (NARA.)

A radiological safety (Rad-Safe) monitor measures residual radioactivity outside a blasted wood-frame house on Yucca Flat. Civil effects testing not only looked at survivability of structures and residents, but also at the utility of equipment following an atomic blast. Though seriously damaged, the automobile pictured was driven away a short time later.

In an effort to assess blast damage to trees and the amount of cover provided by a forest, workers from the Army and the US Forest Service removed 145 ponderosa pines from nearby Mount Charleston and cemented them into concrete blocks to create a simulated grove on Frenchman Flat some 6,500 feet from the 27-kiloton Encore shot on May 8, 1953. (DOE.)

To establish criteria for safe escape distances for airship delivery of antisubmarine warfare special weapons, the Navy in 1957 supplied four ZSG-3 blimps to determine response characteristics when subjected to overpressure from a nuclear detonation. Although shot Franklin on June 2 was a 140-ton fizzle, airship K-77 broke free of its mooring mast, which, together with a tear of the forward ballonet, necessitated deflation of the envelope.

Airship K-40 flies free at an altitude of 300 feet above ground with its tail toward the 19-kiloton fireball from shot Stokes on August 7, 1957. Thermal effects on the blimp's aluminized skin were negligible, but the shock wave delivered 0.75-pounds-per-square inch (psi) overpressure to the delicate fabric. The ensuing results were unsurprising. (USAF.)

The shock wave from Stokes delivered a deathblow to airship K-40. After the blimp buckled and ruptured just forward of the control car, it settled slowly to the ground, nose first. Here, a Navy ground crew inspects the wreck while determining how best to deflate the craft's remaining helium cells.

Deputy for Scientific Programs Alvin C. Graves gazes through a telescope at the results of the March 24, 1953, experimental detonation called Nancy. With him at CP-1 are, from left to right, William Ogle, Civil Effects Test Group director Robert L. Corsbie, and Military Effects Group director Edward B. Doll.

A sign at Gate 200, on the road to the forward areas, warns against handling or removal of blasted debris. NTS managers developed stringent radiological safety protocols to deal with leftover scrap and debris from the atomic tests. All employees and visitors were required to wear personal dosimeter badges designed to record exposure to beta and gamma radiation. (Author's collection.)

Prior to moving into the detonation area after an atomic test in March 1955, Pvt. Roland Lancaster (left) and Cpl. Charles Stout, wearing protective clothing, check equipment and review instructions with Lt. Tom D. Collison, chief of the NTS Rad-Safe group. In the background is a decontamination facility near the Control Point.

Three members of the Rad-Safe group receive their duty assignments from Air Force lieutenant William Bogue. After each detonation, such safety workers surveyed the terrain around ground zero to identify contaminated areas, establish access checkpoints manned by radiation monitors, and set up signs indicating potential radiation exposure levels. Bogue is pointing to a radiation survey map of Area 2.

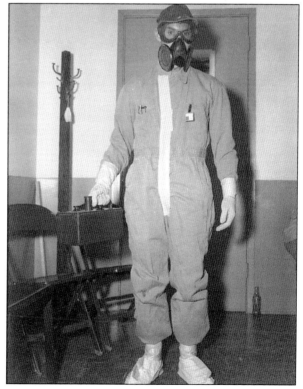

A Rad-Safe monitor wears anticontamination gear during Operation Upshot-Knothole in 1953. He is holding an AN/PDR-T1B Radiac survey meter, which was used to detect the presence of gamma-emitting radioactive materials. Goggles and filtered breathing mask provided protection from radioactive dust. Radiation dosimeters and film badge clipped to his breast pocket provided exposure data.

Robert L. Corsbie (left), director of the Civil Effects Test Group (CETG), and Fred Wilson, assistant to the technical director, take radiation readings from the melted remains of the Apple-2 shot tower on Yucca Flat. In an effort to develop measures for surviving a nuclear detonation, Civil Defense planners studied effects of blast, heat, and residual radiation.

Several days after the 37-kiloton Priscilla shot in June 1957, CETG technicians check the entrance to a family-type bomb shelter that could be easily built in the backyard of a suburban home. This steel-reinforced concrete shelter beneath a mound of earth survived an approximate peak overpressure of 65 psi with relatively little damage.

Three 50-foot-diameter shelters were built on Frenchman Flat for the Priscilla test. These six-inch-thick, reinforced concrete domes were exposed to the blast without the aid of earth cover. Before the test, the entrance is sealed with a steel door. In the background, workers put the finishing touches on several other shelters of varying design and construction.

A Rad-Safe monitor surveys damage to one of three six-inch-thick dome shelters following the 37-kiloton blast. This dome, which was subjected to overpressures ranging from about 20 to 70 psi, was instrumented to determine loads, response, and failure modes. Shelters of greater thickness survived the blast intact or with only slight damage.

Air Force officers colonel Hershel E. "Ted" Parsons (left), deputy for military operations during Operation Plumbbob, and colonel Kenneth D. Coleman, director of the Department of Defense (DOD) Test Group, inspect target structures at Frenchman Flat on June 21, 1957. The railroad bridge in the background had been previously used for the Encore and Grable shots in 1955.

A World War II–vintage Boeing B-17G was flown to the NTS in 1952, instrumented, and subjected to three atomic detonations. Destined for the scrap heap, it was restored by John King of Desert Aviation, Phoenix, Arizona. On May 14, 1965, pilot Abe Sellers flew the B-17, dubbed *Yucca Lady*, off Yucca Flat. She remained flyable into the 21st century, with careers in firefighting and air-show performances.

Numerous new and used automobiles were subjected to atomic blast effects, including this 1953 Ford Mainline V-8 from Operation Doorstep. Most were passenger sedans ranging from 1936 to 1953 models. All major makes were represented. Some tests also included a variety of commercial and government vehicles, such as Postal Service delivery trucks.

An enterprising dealer in Southgate, California, provided this Nash 600 Super for the March 17, 1953, shot. Marked with the words, "DONATED IN THE PUBLIC'S INTEREST" and "THIS CAR WILL GO THRU THE ATOMIC BLAST," the used four-door sedan was publicly displayed at the dealership prior to being shipped to Nevada.

Observers wearing protective goggles prepare to view shot Wasp from the Control Point balcony overlooking Yucca Flat on February 18, 1955. Although dropped from a B-36, the bomb exploded just 762 feet above the ground so as to evaluate the effects of low-altitude detonations. With a yield of merely 1.2 kilotons, Wasp demonstrated a new compact, lightweight implosion system.

Civilian observers gaze in awe at the rising cloud from the 22-kiloton MET shot on April 15, 1955. MET stood for "Military Effects Test," a demonstration of a LASL-designed composite uranium/plutonium bomb core. This test evaluated the destructive effects of nuclear explosions on buildings and military equipment, including drone aircraft flying overhead and vehicles on the ground.

Representatives of the North Atlantic Treaty Organization (NATO) observe the Boltzmann shot on May 28, 1957. Invited guests included visitors from NATO member nations Canada, Denmark, Norway, Italy, West Germany, Britain, France, and the Netherlands. The Boltzmann nuclear device was a lightweight fission warhead weighing less than 300 pounds but capable of producing a 12-kiloton yield.

After doffing protective goggles, representatives of five European nations watch with solemn expressions as an atomic mushroom cloud rises over Yucca Flat on July 24, 1957. The primary purpose of shot Kepler of Operation Plumbbob was the development of components to be used in warheads for intercontinental ballistic missiles.

NTS support director Seth R. Woodruff Jr. (left), test manager James E. Reeves, and scientific advisor Alvin Graves discuss the potential for radioactive fallout in March 1955. Although tests were scheduled for times when the winds were blowing away from most heavily populated areas, particulate debris lofted into the atmosphere by atomic explosions affected populations well beyond NTS boundaries.

As an atomic cloud dissipates over Yucca Flat, dust and debris is spread in several directions by varied wind shear at different altitudes. Despite meteorological precautions, fallout spread over adjacent regions. Parts of Nevada, Utah, and Arizona took the brunt of it, but radioactive residue was tracked across most parts of the country from coast to coast.

From the parking lot at News Nob, the cloud from shot Smoky rises against the dawn sky on August 31, 1957. Reporters and news photographers were 17 miles from the 44-kiloton detonation, but Desert Rock troops occupied trenches within 4,500 yards of the blast. Some of them later marched to within 300 feet of the melted tower remains, where radiation levels were very high. The cloud drifted northeast, depositing fallout on several Utah communities as well as on Zion National Park. The upper levels of Smoky's radioactive plume spread out, eventually passing into Canada through North Dakota and Minnesota. Portions later returned across the northern tip of Maine before passing over parts of New York and New Hampshire and eventually heading straight for Boston, Massachusetts. Lower portions of the cloud stem meandered over parts of Wyoming, South Dakota, Missouri, Kentucky, Tennessee, and North Carolina before leaving the continent near Norfolk, Virginia.

Army soldiers at Buckboard Mesa prepare to fire a dummy XM388 Davy Crockett round in preparation for the Little Feller I shot on July 17, 1962. The smallest nuclear weapon ever produced by the United States, the XM388 projectile was designed to carry a W54 atomic fission warhead with a selectable explosive yield from 10 to 250 tons TNT. (NARA.)

For Little Feller I, a live XM388 was fired from a 155-mm recoilless rifle and set to detonate less than 40 feet above the ground approximately 1.7 miles from the launch point, with a yield of 18 tons. Soldiers then performed simulated tactical mancuvers. Notably, this was the last atmospheric nuclear test in Nevada. (NARA.)

Two

UNDERGROUND TESTING

The Area 12 camp was used to support miners working in the tunnels in Rainier Mesa and Pahute Mesa as well as those working at the extreme northwest end of the NTS. The camp provided overnight accommodations for more than 600 people, a 320-seat cafeteria, recreation hall, theater, heavy-duty equipment repair shop, first-aid facility, supply depot, and office trailers.

Workers at the entrance portal to a tunnel in the side of Rainier Mesa prepare for the first completely subterranean full-scale nuclear test in September 1957. Underground testing offered opportunities to eliminate fallout and conceal test effects from unauthorized observers. The primary purpose of this shot was to evaluate containment techniques and methods for detection of underground nuclear testing activities.

Arthur Morse (right) of the CBS television program *See It Now* interviews Dale Nielsen, general manager of the University of California Radiation Laboratory, Nevada operations, inside the Rainier shot tunnel diagnostics room. Scientific equipment within this chamber would collect and preserve data from the first underground nuclear explosion at the NTS.

Dust rises from the side of Rainier Mesa on September 19, 1957, following the first contained underground nuclear explosion. The 1.7-kiloton Rainier event was announced in advance so that seismic stations throughout the United States and Canada could attempt to record a signal. Results of this test affected the future of nuclear arms control and the conduct of nuclear testing. (LLNL.)

Radiation-safety monitors check the air at the mouth of the Rainier tunnel a few minutes after detonation. They detected no trace of radiation here or, subsequently, within the first two sections of the tunnel. Collapse of the deepest part of the shot tunnel at the time of detonation completely contained both blast and residual radiation.

In the Rainier diagnostics room, workers recover a core sample from the shot area. Radiochemistry analysis of these samples enabled scientists to develop an understanding of underground explosion phenomenology, information that provided a basis for subsequent decisions leading to the 1963 Limited Test Ban Treaty, which banned atmospheric nuclear weapon tests.

Workers measure radiation from a core sample following the Rainer event. Determining the distribution of radioactive material was key to establishing dimensions of the shot cavity. The Rainier cavity was found to be approximately 55 feet in diameter. Another result of this test was the establishment of an international array of seismic detectors for monitoring nuclear test activities worldwide.

The N-Tunnel complex was one of several passages mined into Rainier Mesa. A total of 22 nuclear tests were conducted here from 1967 to 1992, as well as 11 high-explosive shots that included a stemming test, pre-shot experiment, two seismic non-proliferation experiments, and seven tests made to evaluate damage done to a tunnel system by a penetrator weapon and to assess the amount of time and materials needed for repairs.

This system was used to collect samples of radioactive gases following the 0.072-kiloton Tamalpais shot on October 8, 1958. An evacuated pipe leading to the shot chamber about 125 feet away drew off samples of gas and dust produced by the blast. Eight of ten tanks recovered contained useful material. Two workers were slightly injured in an accident during reentry in which hydrogen gas ignited in the tunnel.

T-Tunnel was used for six nuclear weapon effects tests and one high-explosive test between 1970 and 1987. This complex consists of a main access drift with two blast containment structures, a gas-seal plug, and a gas-seal door. T-Tunnel was mothballed in 1993 to preserve the passage for future resumption of testing should it occur.

A reentry team, dressed in anticontamination clothing and self-contained breathing apparatus, prepares to enter T-Tunnel on May 13, 1970, eight days after the detonation of Mint Leaf. Radiation levels were expected to be significant because gases had begun seeping through the tunnel-stemming material toward the portal 34 minutes after detonation. This seepage continued until the shot cavity collapsed 62 hours later.

A team of miners examines the working face of a tunnel deep inside Rainier Mesa. Decades spent carving away at the geology of the NTS has resulted in the creation of a unique subterranean experimental complex. Geological stability and a controlled environment make these tunnels ideal for a variety of scientific projects. Some 20,000 linear feet of accessible underground passages are available for experiments within the nearly 50 miles of tunnels at the NTS. Within these passages, distinctive engineering installations range from massive mechanical, vacuum, cryogenic, and communications systems to the most sophisticated power and instrument cabling and wiring systems. Mining experts have perfected tunneling technology to safely and efficiently excavate tunnels as large as 25 feet in diameter through solid rock. Caverns as high as 98 feet are not uncommon. Unique challenges posed by NTS requirements led to development of techniques, equipment, and safety procedures never before required in the industry.

At the height of nuclear testing, mining inside Rainier Mesa was an around-the-clock operation. Shown here is an instrumentation alcove in P-Tunnel during early stages of excavation. Diagnostic equipment would be installed here to gather scientific data from weapons-effects experiments; readings would be taken within less than a millionth of a second after detonation. Later, the equipment would be recovered and reused in other tunnel tests.

In a first for the NTS, two shots—Huron Landing and Diamond Ace—were fired simultaneously in the same tunnel complex on September 23, 1982. The two devices, each with yields less than 20 kilotons, were only 40 feet apart. Radiation from the blast passed through line-of-sight pipes to instrumentation within this test chamber, 970 feet from the detonation point for Huron Landing.

Line-of-sight pipes to measure the effects of blast-produced radiation on military hardware are fabricated inside tunnels at Rainier Mesa. These tapered pipes could be anywhere from several inches to 27 feet in diameter. Experiments were located within test chambers 900 to 2,000 feet from the detonation point. These tests helped ensure the survivability of military equipment in a nuclear environment.

During the Diamond Sculls shot on July 20, 1972, radiation traveled 2,000 feet down a tapered horizontal line-of-sight pipe to this 27-foot-diameter vacuum chamber. A full-scale missile was placed in the chamber to see what effect intensive radiation from a nuclear blast would have on an intercontinental ballistic missile passing through the fringes of outer space. Fast closure doors in the pipe stopped flying debris and protected the experiments.

At left, Rowan Drilling Company's Emsco 1500 heavy-duty drilling rig bores a 64-inch-diameter, 3,850-foot-deep emplacement hole for the Jorum test, detonated on September 16, 1969. On the right, two other government-owned rigs, operated by Reynolds Electrical and Engineering Company, drill auxiliary and exploratory holes for test instrumentation and site characterization. (LLNL.)

Here, workers install a post-shot drilling blowout preventer, a device used to preclude the escape of radioactive effluents into the atmosphere during post-shot reentry operations. Containing the nuclear blast and its radioactive byproducts underground required the development of new science and technologies that came to be known collectively as "Caging the Dragon."

A worker checks core samples at a potential underground test site on Yucca Flat to evaluate the subsurface environment and its acceptability as storage media for highly radioactive solid wastes. Note that the worker's hard hat is decorated with decals commemorating various nuclear test shots, including Husky Ace and Husky Pup.

Test preparations are underway at Area 2 in the late 1960s. Over a 10-year span, 20 shots were fired in drill holes within this 4,500-foot-diameter circle. Preparations are being made at the circle's center for Potrero, which was not fired until April 1974. Area 12 Camp is visible at upper left. (LLNL.)

Large diameter bits were used for Big-Hole drilling at the NTS. In 1981, workers drilled 20 Big Holes, 64 to 96 inches in diameter, to an average depth of 1,590 feet. These holes were drilled at a rate in excess of 100 feet per day and with a bottom offset of only slightly more than one foot per 1,000 feet of depth.

Weighing about 300,000 pounds, a flat-bottom bit with 17 cutters could drill a 1,000-foot hole in 20 days. Every 100 hours, the drill string had to be completely removed from the hole to enable routine maintenance and to replace the drill bit with a rebuilt bit or a new one.

The EMSCO 3000 was one of the largest drill rigs used at the NTS. To drill an emplacement hole with this equipment, a 120-inch-diameter bit and drill string was used to bore to a depth of 65 feet. After constructing a 98-inch concrete casing, the remainder of the hole would be drilled with a 96-inch bit and string.

AEC chairman Glenn T. Seaborg (right) visits the mobile instrumentation tower for Milk Shake on March 16, 1968, nine days before the 10-kiloton shot was fired beneath Frenchman Flat. The device, supplied by Lawrence Radiation Laboratory, was emplaced in a 66-inch-diameter cased hole drilled to a depth of 867 feet. A vertical line-of-site pipe connected the detonation point to a test chamber in the tower. (LLNL.)

A device diagnostics rack suspended within the emplacement tower. The tower structure protects this assembly during installation and calibration of test instruments. The rack and device canister will be lowered into the hole, then the tower will be disassembled and the hole backfilled with a combination of sand, gravel, concrete, and epoxy that stems the hole to ensure containment of the nuclear explosion.

Firing-signal and instrumentation cables surround the base of an emplacement tower on Yucca Flat. Inside the tower, technicians assemble a seven-foot-wide instrumentation rack and attach the nuclear device. The entire assembly would have weighed around 350,000 pounds at the beginning of descent. As cables were fed downhole, the assembly would have weighed 500,000 pounds by the time it reached firing depth.

The Handley event canister, including both the device and diagnostics rack, is lowered into a drill hole at Pahute Mesa. This shot, with a yield of 1.9 megatons, was conducted on March 26, 1970. The platform at right, nicknamed "Little Joe," is a cable chute used to guide the timing, firing, and diagnostic cables down the hole without crimping.

A crane lowers the Cabra event canister into a 1,778-foot-deep hole on Pahute Mesa. Detonated on March 26, 1983, this 45-kiloton shot was one of several experiments to test the ability to produce a nuclear-pumped X-ray laser. One of the most heavily instrumented tests ever conducted at the NTS, it required more than 213 downhole cables and more than 300 oscilloscopes to record data.

CP-1 served as the principal command and firing center for 100 atmospheric and 828 underground nuclear tests. The windowless building has eight-inch-thick reinforced-concrete walls. All the structures in this area were designed to withstand an increase in atmospheric pressure of 0.6 psi in anticipation of the windblast effects from atmospheric detonations. (DNA.)

Personnel manning consoles in the main control room at CP-1 included the test coordinator, meteorologist, medical and scientific advisers, and a representative of the Environmental Protection Agency. A computer-controlled countdown began about five to 15 minutes prior to detonation, with the firing signal being sent to the device via microwave signal.

Instrumentation cables fan out from the top of an 811-foot-deep emplacement hole on Yucca Flat. Diagnostic signals from the blast, a 10-kiloton shot called Tapestry that was fired on May 12, 1966, were sent to scientific equipment located in the trailers at upper left, where cameras recorded oscilloscope readings and other data. (LLNL.)

Underground nuclear detonations vaporized surrounding rock, leaving a subterranean cavity hundreds of feet across. Within minutes or hours, the overlying rock and soil collapsed, leaving a rubble-filled chimney. This usually resulted in formation of a bowl-shaped subsidence crater at the surface. The moment of subsidence is seen here following the 8-kiloton Backswing shot on May 14, 1964. (LLNL.)

An aerial view of subsidence craters dotting Yucca Flat resembles the surface of the moon. Crater size varied depending on many factors including explosive yield, depth of burial, and local geology. Subsidence craters ranged from 200 to 2,000 feet in diameter and from a few feet to 200 feet deep. In some cases, no crater ever formed.

Workers enter a subsidence crater on October 12, 1967, two weeks after the 160-kiloton Zaza shot. Post-shot operations included inspection and characterization of the crater and drilling to collect samples from the vicinity of the shot cavity. Radioactive specimens provided critical data with regard to performance of the explosive device.

Two UH-1N helicopters fly over the cratered landscape of Yucca Flat. Assigned to Detachment 1, 57th Fighter Weapons Wing, at Indian Springs, six of these choppers were used for test support, security sweeps, aerial photography, and radiological monitoring. Later redesignated the 4460th Helicopter Squadron, this unit was inactivated in 1988.

Final test preparations are underway on Yucca Flat. Note the proximity of diagnostic trailers (left), emplacement tower, and cranes to subsidence craters from earlier underground tests. Multiple shots might be performed in the same geographical areas at different times; holes for new tests could be drilled very close to sites of previous tests.

On July 6, 1962, the AEC detonated a 104-kiloton thermonuclear device near the north end of Yucca Flat. The large "bubble" of rising earth, approximately 600 to 800 feet in diameter at the time of this photograph, rose to a height of nearly 300 feet within three seconds of detonation. The plume at the top of the bubble is sand used to plug the emplacement hole.

The Sedan shot was the first excavation experiment in Plowshare, an ambitious program to develop peaceful uses for nuclear explosives. Applications included planned future excavation of canals and harbors, building dams, cutting highway passes through mountains, and removing overburden in mining operations. The seismic energy released by Sedan was equivalent to a 4.75-magnitude earthquake.

The Sedan shot displaced 12 million tons of earth. Fired 635 feet beneath the surface, the optimum depth for cratering at the planned yield, the detonation resulted in a crater approximately 1,200 feet in diameter with a depth of 320 feet. Entered into the National Register of Historic Places in 1994, the crater attracts more than 10,000 visitors each year. (LLNL.)

Workers in protective garb survey the lip of Sedan crater. The device used was a thermonuclear design; fission contributed less than 30 percent of the total yield. The shot was considered relatively "clean" from a radiological standpoint in that approximately 95 percent of residual radioactivity was trapped underground. Most of the small amount of radioactive material ejected from the crater was deposited nearby with the fallback of earth.

Shot Pliers of Operation Mandrel, on August 27, 1969, had a yield of 10 kilotons. Scientific instruments were installed within a 100-foot-tall, 200-ton experimental tower that took several months to assemble. The tower was mounted on railroad tracks so it could be slid out of the way before the subsidence crater formed.

Little more than a minute after the Pliers underground nuclear detonation, the instrument tower was pulled along tracks by cables from above the detonation point. About 23 minutes later, the ground collapsed into the cavity caused by the detonation, producing a 350-foot-wide, 50-foot-deep crater. A slight accidental release of radioactivity was detected onsite only.

Huron King was a test to study the effects of electromagnetic pulse (EMP) on satellites in space. The 1967 Outer Space Treaty prohibited deployment or use of nuclear weapons in space, so scientists brought space down to Earth. A test satellite was suspended inside a 50-ton vacuum chamber on tractor treads and installed on top of a 1,000-foot vertical line-of-site pipe at surface ground zero.

When the Huron King device detonated with a yield of less than 20 kilotons, the satellite was exposed to EMP for a fraction of a second. Mechanical closures immediately sealed the pipe to prevent the shock wave from reaching the delicate spacecraft, and the test chamber was disconnected from the pipe and moved to safety before the ground subsided into a crater.

Petrel, a 1.3-kiloton neutron physics experiment sponsored by LASL, was detonated on June 11, 1965, in Area 3. Prior to the test, a special tower was constructed above the emplacement hole to accommodate nine different experiments for measuring the fission cross-sections of various isotopes of plutonium, uranium, and americium. (LANL.)

LANL scientists fired the 1.3 kiloton shot Parrot on December 16, 1964. Although the physics tower and instruments withstood subsequent surface subsidence with little damage, data produced by Parrot were of questionable accuracy due to neutrons reflecting from the bottom of the explosion cavity, causing "ghost" peaks on the measurements. (LANL.)

Containment of underground nuclear explosions was not always successful. Blanca, a 22-kiloton tunnel shot on October 30, 1958, vented through the overburden at the edge of Rainier Mesa. The ensuing dust cloud containing highly radioactive material rose 580 feet and drifted off in a westerly direction. Two months later, all of the pinyon and juniper trees within 1,000 feet of the vent had died.

Detonated 910 feet beneath Yucca Flat, the 10-kiloton Baneberry shot on December 18, 1970, vented unexpectedly, spewing a radioactive plume that was tracked as far as the Canadian border. The venting may have resulted from a combination of water-saturated clay, a buried hard-rock scarp increasing the explosion's force, and a nearby fault that provided a pathway for escaping gases.

In a scene of unprecedented cooperation in the Cold War era, flags of the United States and USSR fly side by side atop a tower at the NTS during the first of two Joint Verification Experiments in 1988. Russian scientists observed the Kearsarge shot and US personnel witnessed the Shagan test in the Soviet Union later that year. Both experiments demonstrated technologies for verifying the yields of nuclear tests.

Divider, the last full-scale underground test of a nuclear explosive device, was conducted on September 23, 1992. Shortly afterward, Pres. George H.W. Bush signed legislation decreeing a nine-month moratorium on US nuclear weapons testing, a mandate that has been extended by every subsequent US president. Scientists have since developed innovative tools and methods to keep the nation's nuclear stockpile safe, secure, and effective without underground testing.

Three

BEYOND THE BOMB

Jointly managed by the AEC and NASA from 1959 to 1973, the Nuclear Rocket Development Station (NRDS) at Jackass Flat was the nation's primary facility for conducting full-scale tests of nuclear propulsion systems for spacecraft. The program originated with LASL's Rover project to develop a nuclear-powered engine for Air Force missiles, but with the creation of NASA in 1958, the focus shifted to development of engines for use in advanced, long-duration deep space missions. Researchers at the NRDS tested a variety of reactors and engines, starting with the Kiwi series developed for Rover and culminating in the Nuclear Engine for Rocket Vehicle Application (NERVA) series. The Rover and NERVA programs were cancelled for a variety of reasons, including environmental concerns, loss of public and political interest in a manned spaceflight in the wake of Apollo, and the growing use low-cost unmanned, robotic space probes.

Kiwi was named after the small, flightless bird. This first phase of Project Rover consisted of a series of non-flyable engine test articles, with primary focus on improving hydrogen-cooled reactor technology. Successful testing of Kiwi-A was considered proof that nuclear rocket engines were not only feasible but highly reliable and advantageous for space travel.

Kiwi-A was fired for the first and only time on July 1, 1959, with a burn time of 30 seconds and maximum power output of 70 megawatts. Between 1959 and 1964, a total of eight Kiwi reactors were built and tested. This series eventually demonstrated a 990-megawatt maximum power output.

More than three-dozen scientists, engineers, and observers crowd the NRDS Control Point during a test. Control room personnel consisted of about 20 operators under the direction of a chief test operator, who received his orders from the test director. Others present included the data acquisition team, test-cell monitoring team, Rad-Safe personnel, and technicians on hand to repair any malfunctioning equipment.

LASL director Norris Bradbury (left) examines the Kiwi-B4A reactor. The Kiwi-B series increased power by tenfold while maintaining the compact size of the Kiwi-A series. The Kiwi reactors experienced a problem with internal vibrations that fractured portions of the fuel elements, but LASL scientists eventually resolved this issue during tests of the Kiwi-B4A.

Pres. John F. Kennedy, the only sitting US president to visit the NTS, tours one of the NRDS test stands on December 8, 1962. Those to his left include AEC chairman Glenn Seaborg, Nevada senator Howard Cannon, Space Nuclear Propulsion Office manager Harold. B. Finger, and LASL test director Alvin Graves. Kennedy arrived at the NRDS following an hour-long aerial tour over Frenchman Flat and Yucca Flat by helicopter from Indian Springs. In a speech several days later, he acknowledged that advances in nuclear propulsion would not play a role in the first lunar landings, but he suggested that the technology had great potential for use on future manned expeditions to the moon and Mars. Because a nuclear thermal rocket is capable of releasing ten million times the energy of a conventional chemical rocket, nuclear-powered spacecraft could cut interplanetary transit times by half or better. (LANL.)

The Kiwi Transient Nuclear Test, or Kiwi-TNT, on January 12, 1965, simulated a worst-case scenario of a reactor accident on the launch pad. The reactor assembly, including the core and pressure vessel, was a modified Kiwi-B4. After being moved to a remote location via special railroad car, the reactor was allowed to go supercritical, vaporizing a significant portion of the core. (LANL.)

The Kiwi-TNT explosion vaporized approximately 5 to 20 percent of the reactor core and released a significant amount of radioactive effluents into the atmosphere, though less than predicted. Safety experts estimated that anyone within 100 feet would have died on the spot from blast effects, anyone within 400 feet would have received a lethal radiation dose, and anyone within 1,000 feet would have received an unhealthy dose.

NRDS workers move the Phoebus-1B reactor to a test site at Jackass Flat in 1967. The prime mover for the test cart was a battery-operated, radio-controlled locomotive, dubbed the "Jackass & Western Railroad." The Phoebus series was the second phase of Project Rover and was focused on achieving more power than was possible with the Kiwi units while maintaining maximum thrust for longer durations. (LANL.)

The NERVA XE-Prime is pushed to the test stand via the Jackass & Western Railroad. Although similar to several earlier reactor assemblies, the XE-Prime was the first nuclear rocket engine to be tested with components assembled in a flight-ready configuration. The engine was oriented to fire downward into a reduced-pressure compartment to partially simulate firing in a vacuum. (LANL.)

Workers supervise movement of the XE-Prime toward the test stand. The object in the foreground is one of two clamshell shields that enveloped the engine and were evacuated of atmosphere prior to firing to simulate the vacuum of space. Test objectives included verifying engine system operational feasibility and demonstrating completely automatic engine startup. (NASA.)

Technicians install the NERVA XE-Prime on the test stand in December 1967. During a series of tests from December 1968 through September 1969, the XE-Prime was fired 24 times using liquid hydrogen fuel. The engine had a nominal thrust of 55,430 pounds and a power rating of 1,140 megawatts. (NASA.)

The XE-Prime experimental engine awaits firing in Engine Test Stand No. 1 (ETS-1) at Jackass Flat. This facility included a pressure vessel containing 70,000 gallons of liquid hydrogen, installed in the superstructure above the engine firing position. The last of the NERVA engines, the XE-prime was tested under simulated space vacuum conditions. ETS-1 was configured for vertical, downward firing of the engine in a simulated flight-stage assembly. Following a series of cold-flow tests in 1968, nuclear-powered testing of the XE-Prime began on March 20, 1969, and continued through September 11. Researchers logged a total of 115 minutes of operation (including a full-power run at 1,100 megawatts for 820 seconds), starting and stopping 28 times. Objectives included testing start-up characteristics under different control modes, evaluation of engine performance, and investigation of shutdown and pulse-cooling operations. At the time, NASA officials felt these tests confirmed that a nuclear rocket engine was suitable for space flight applications. (NASA.)

Project Pluto began in 1957 as a joint project between the Air Force and the AEC to develop nuclear ramjet engines for low-flying, supersonic cruise missiles with virtually unlimited range. Lawrence Radiation Laboratory in Livermore, California, designed and built the Tory II-A experimental reactor to demonstrate concept feasibility. It was successfully tested during a brief ground run on May 14, 1961.

The 500-megawatt Tory II-C represented a near-flight-ready engine prototype that could potentially be mated to an airframe. It was successfully tested during several ground runs in 1964, including one lasting five minutes and producing the equivalent of 35,000 pounds of thrust. Environmental and political concerns, however, ultimately doomed Pluto to cancellation. (LLNL.)

In 1955, the AEC announced construction of Watertown Airstrip, a small airfield at Groom Dry Lake, just off the northeast corner of the NTS. Facilities included a 5,000-foot runway, control tower, three hangars, warehouses, administrative buildings, dining hall, three-dozen trailers, and a water tower. The base's few amenities included a movie theater and volleyball court. The dry lake bed also served as a landing field. (RRI.)

Although officials claimed that Watertown's fleet of Lockheed U-2 aircraft were assigned to the National Advisory Committee for Aeronautics for use in high-altitude weather research, they were actually part of a training program for CIA and Air Force reconnaissance pilots. Watertown's proximity to the atomic proving ground helped shield the operation from public view. In 1959, the facility and its environs were redesignated Area 51. (CIA.)

By 1964, little remained of the original Watertown facilities. Under CIA management, Area 51 had grown into a permanent full-scale air base with more than a dozen hangars for test and support aircraft, new administrative buildings and control tower, improved personnel accommodations, a fuel farm, and an 8,600-foot-long concrete runway. (RRI.)

During the 1960s, Area 51 was home to the CIA's Oxcart project, in which Lockheed built and tested a high-speed, high-altitude spy plane capable of achieving speeds of more than 2,000 miles per hour and altitudes up to 90,000 feet. In 1977, the facility was transferred to the Air Force for use in a variety of special projects that continue to this day. (RRI.)

The Experimental Farm facility in Area 15 was established in 1963 to conduct fallout-related metabolism studies on animals and crops. The farm included a herd of dairy cows, an irrigated agricultural area for growing forage, milking facilities, and laboratories for collection and analysis of specimens. The facility was mostly decommissioned at the end of 1981. (NARA.)

Ken Case, the "Atomic Cowboy," shows off the AEC brand used to mark cattle at the NTS. Case oversaw a 100-cow beef herd used since the mid-1950s for an investigation program that studied uptake and retention of radionuclides by animals grazing on forage contaminated by decades of atmospheric nuclear tests, as well as by fallout from accidental or planned releases of radioactivity from underground tests.

In November 1970, NASA Apollo 16 astronauts Charles Duke (left) and John Young explored a crater created by the 31-kiloton Schooner device two years earlier. The terrain and geology closely matched that of South Ray crater near their intended landing site on the lunar surface. For added realism, the astronauts wore suits similar to what they would be wearing on the moon. (NASA.)

Apollo 16 astronauts drive a Lunar Roving Vehicle in the vicinity of Schooner crater. Several groups of Apollo astronauts trained at the NTS, carrying out geological and geophysical studies in preparation for expeditions to the moon. This allowed them to study features that proved common on the lunar surface, such as secondary craters and glass-coated rocks. (NASA.)

The Climax Spent Fuel Test was conducted from 1980 to 1983 inside a deep tunnel mined into a granite formation to evaluate safe and reliable packaging, transport, short-term storage, and retrieval of spent reactor fuel. A remotely controlled underground transfer vehicle was used to emplace and retrieve canisters from individual storage boreholes.

Eleven canisters containing spent fuel elements were lowered into steel-lined holes in the tunnel floor and capped with 5,000-pound concrete plugs. When the canisters were in place, readings on the top of the plugs were below natural radiation levels from the surrounding granite. Parallel tunnels with electric heaters simulated the heat from radiation decay that normally would occur in a large-scale repository.

The Area 3 Disposal Site is used for bulk and packaged low-level radioactive waste from cleanup of surface contamination on the NTS and from off-site waste generators. Four subsidence craters with excavated areas in between make up two oval-shaped landfill units. Much of the waste material consists of debris from atmospheric nuclear testing.

Crates of low-level radioactive waste are stacked in a shallow burial pit at the Area 5 Radioactive Waste Management Site on Frenchman Flat. Established in 1961, this site is used for disposal of onsite- and offsite-generated low-level waste and onsite-generated low-level mixed waste, as well as for storage of transuranic waste. (Author's collection.)

Yucca Mountain in Area 25 was selected for exploratory studies of techniques for deep-underground disposal of high-level radioactive waste. In 1994, a 25-foot-diameter Tunnel Boring Machine (TBM) began excavating a five-mile-long tunnel. Custom-built for the Yucca Mountain Project (YMP), the TBM, mapping gantry, and trailing gear stretched more than the length of a football field.

In April 1997, after two-and-a-half years without a serious injury to workers, the TBM emerged at the South Portal of the U-shaped main tunnel at YMP's Exploratory Studies Facility. The 860-ton TBM pulled 13 special railcars behind it that allowed scientists to study rock samples and take detailed pictures of the tunnels.

The YMP main tunnel's scale dwarfs a worker. By 2008, Yucca Mountain had become one of the most studied geological formations in the world at a cost of $9 billion. Shipments of spent reactor fuel were originally scheduled to begin in 1998, but ongoing political battles in Congress have indefinitely delayed plans to use the depository for its intended purpose.

In a 150-foot-long full-scale repository simulation alcove, technicians from Bechtel SAIC filled containers with electrical heaters to determine how the mountain would react to the heat of nuclear waste. A complex array of instruments gave scientists information about heating effects as well as data on how rainwater might move from the mountain's surface through fractures and faults down into the rock.

On August 23, 2010, the National Nuclear Security Administration (NNSA) announced that the NTS was officially renamed the Nevada National Security Site, abbreviated as NNSS or N2S2, to reflect the test site's expanded mission beyond support of the US nuclear stockpile. The NNSS also provides a location for evaluating sensor technologies and methods of detecting, characterizing, and monitoring nuclear weapon–related activities for arms control and nonproliferation purposes; management of the NNSA's nuclear emergency response efforts; and support of other federal agency activities, such as remote imaging, chemical/biological projects, military training, and special projects. The Nonproliferation Test and Evaluation Complex in Area 5 is used to conduct low-level, controlled chemical releases in an open environment to simulate emissions from nuclear weapons production plants. The Area 12 Camp and tunnel complex are currently used to conduct experiments and training in support of military and intelligence entities as well as NNSA emergency response and nonproliferation research. (Ken Lund.)

Following the 1992 moratorium on underground nuclear weapons testing, US weapons labs implemented alternate experimental methods for certifying the nation's nuclear weapons stockpile. Among these was the Joint Actinide Shock Physics Experimental Research (JASPER) facility, where scientists generate and measure data pertaining to the properties of nuclear materials at high shock pressures, temperatures, and strain rates that approximate those occurring in nuclear weapons.

Scientists make adjustments to the JASPER Primary Target Chamber with the Secondary Confinement Chamber. Experiment results are used for code refinement, permitting better predictive capability and ensuring confidence in the US nuclear stockpile. JASPER is a multi-organizational research facility, hosting scientists from Lawrence Livermore National Laboratory, Los Alamos National Laboratory, Sandia National Laboratories, Bechtel Nevada, and the US Department of Energy's National Nuclear Security Administration.

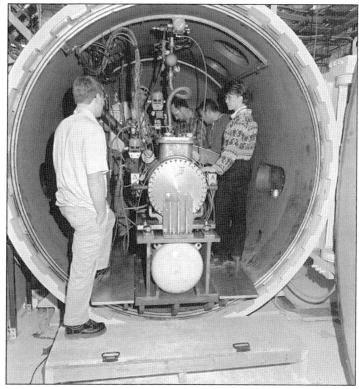

Los Alamos scientists at the Big Explosive Experimental Facility (BEEF) in Area 4 conduct Watusi, a spectacular high-explosives experiment with a yield equivalent to about 37,000 pounds of TNT. Several underground structures at the BEEF, left over from atmospheric testing, have been modified to serve as a hydrodynamic test facility for detonations of very large conventional HE charges.

The Device Assembly Facility (DAF) in Area 6 is used to support activities related to nuclear test readiness and science-based stockpile stewardship. The DAF provides a modern, safe, and secure facility for NTS nuclear explosive handling operations such as assembling subcritical experiments, supporting test readiness exercises, training laboratory weapons engineers and technicians, and developing improved surveillance technology for aging stockpile weapons.

The Radiological Assistance Program (RAP) provides first-responder training to those charged with protecting the health and safety of the general public and the environment in the event of a radiological accident or act of terrorism. RAP-trained personnel assist other federal, state, tribal, and local agencies in the detection, identification and analysis, and response to events involving the use of nuclear materials.

The Counter Terrorism Operations Support facility in Area 1 was the site of several atmospheric nuclear tests: Tumbler-Snapper Easy, Upshot-Knothole Simon, Teapot Apple-2, and Plumbbob Galileo. This unique location allows for the conduct of realistic RAP first-responder training in a radiologically contaminated environment. Here, trainees learn how to take immediate, decisive action to prevent or mitigate terrorist use of radiological weapons of mass destruction.

Since October 2010, robots have been used to beef up security patrols in some of the more remote portions of the sprawling desert installation. Known as Mobile Detection Assessment Response Systems (MDARS), these robots are operated remotely from a command center at Mercury. Onboard sensors and real-time video allow the operator to see intruders or suspect activity.

NTS security systems for the 21st century also included the Advanced Concept Armored Vehicle, Model II, or ACAV II, with remotely operated weapon systems. The ACAV II pictured is a modified Ford F-350 Super Duty 4x4 pickup truck with thermal imaging systems and closed-circuit television viewing for the driver and gunner as well as a platform equipped with a thermal imaging scope.

Security personnel block the road to Mercury as about 150 people peacefully demonstrated on May 28, 2006, to stop the planned Divine Strake high-explosive test. More than 40 were cited for trespassing on federal land when they attempted entry. The test site has been a magnet for antinuclear and antiwar protests since it was established. (James P. McMahon.)

Addressing security forces across the test site boundary line on October 9, 2011, a headman of the Western Shoshone Nation denounces the theft of lands once occupied by Native Americans and the contamination of the landscape from nuclear testing. Members of the Catholic Worker Gathering and Nevada Desert Experience joined the Shoshone to offer their support. (Chris Nelson.)

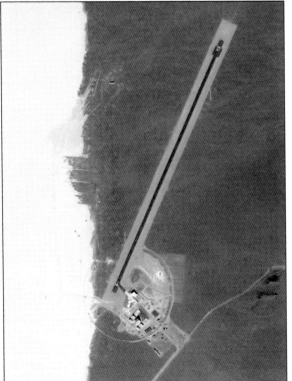

An unpaved airstrip on the clay surface of Yucca Lake once supported atomic testing activities. A newer airfield, the Yucca Lake Aerial Operations Facility, was built for an undisclosed government customer in 2002. Both airstrips have since been used to support the development of classified unmanned aircraft system (UAS) technologies. (Doc Searls.)

The Yucca Lake airfield consists of a 5,000-foot asphalt runway and four hangars of varying sizes, including one with clamshell doors that is characteristic of UAS operations. These hangars could potentially accommodate more than a dozen aircraft. Chase planes and personnel transport aircraft also use the facility, which can accommodate up to 80 people. (USGS.)

Lockheed Martin secretly tested its P-175 Polecat UAS technology demonstrator at Yucca Lake in 2005. The aircraft is seen here near the end of the unpaved runway marked on the lake bed's surface. The stealthy craft was designed to verify cost-effective rapid-prototyping and manufacturing techniques, aerodynamic performance for sustained high-altitude operations, and autonomous flight controls. (LMSW.)

The P-175 soars over the NTS during a 2005 test flight. The Polecat made two successful flights from the lake bed airstrip in Area 6, attaining a maximum altitude of 15,000 feet. Unfortunately, the P-175 crashed on December 18, 2006, when a ground-equipment failure led to inadvertent activation of the aircraft's flight-termination system. (LMSW.)

A family of kit foxes peers from a culvert at a construction site. Far from being a blasted nuclear wasteland, the NTS is a bountiful wildlife preserve inhabited by a wide variety of animals ranging from kangaroo rats to mule deer and wild horses, from centipedes to rattlesnakes, and from bats to golden eagles.

Although not native, small herds of wild horses roam the higher elevations of the NTS. In addition, more than 30 species of birds have been identified on the test site, including robins, hawks, quail, and chukars. No hunting is permitted on the NTS, and any employee who purposely harms an animal their faces dismissal.

Prehistoric petroglyphs in Fortymile Canyon may be 2,000 to 4,000 years old. The earliest cultural remains recorded at the NTS date back more than 10,000 years. More recently, the area was home to widely scattered groups of hunter-gatherers known today as the Southern Paiute and Western Shoshone. Archaeologists continue to perform surveys and data recovery efforts at the NTS.

A cabin overlooking Tippipah Spring is one of numerous historic sites on the NTS. Euro-American explorers passed through the area in 1849. Four decades later, prospectors established several small mining districts, and the short-lived town of Wahmonie was founded in 1928. Eventually, this land was absorbed into the Las Vegas Bombing and Gunnery Range at the start of World War II.

DISCOVER THOUSANDS OF LOCAL HISTORY BOOKS FEATURING MILLIONS OF VINTAGE IMAGES

Arcadia Publishing, the leading local history publisher in the United States, is committed to making history accessible and meaningful through publishing books that celebrate and preserve the heritage of America's people and places.

Find more books like this at
www.arcadiapublishing.com

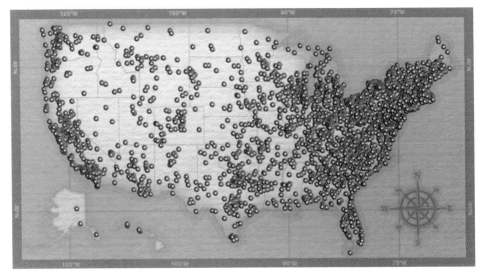

Search for your hometown history, your old stomping grounds, and even your favorite sports team.